FILL IN THE
SPANK

FILL-IN-THE-BLANK EROTIC SHORT STORIES!

BY THE EDITORS OF CLEIS PRESS

CLEiS
PRESS

Published in the United States by Cleis Press, an imprint of Start Midnight, LLC, 221 River Street, Ninth Floor, Hoboken, NJ 07030.

Printed in the United States.
Cover design: Jennifer Do
Cover image: Shutterstock
Text design: Frank Wiedemann

First Edition.
10 9 8 7 6 5 4 3 2 1

Trade paper ISBN: 978-1-62778-309-5

FILL IN THE
SPANK

TABLE OF CONTENTS

FILL IN THE SPANK

ANIMAL SOUNDS
Fill in the Spank:

Body Part: _____

Animal: _____

Silly Sound: _____

Piece of Furniture: _____

Animal: _____

Sexy Adjective: _____

Animal: _____

Noun: _____

Body Part: _____

Verb Ending in -ING: _____

Verb Ending in -ING: _____

As I reclined on the bed, I could feel my _____ quivering.
BODY PART

"Growl at me like a(n) _____," he said. I
ANIMAL

scrunched up my nose and let out a loud _____.
SILLY SOUND

The sound of my desire drove him wild, and he hopped off

the _____, creeping toward me like a(n)
PIECE OF FURNITURE

_____, his _____ body ready
ANIMAL **SEXY ADJECTIVE**

to pounce. His hair was shaggy, like a(n) _____'s,
ANIMAL

and when he finally sprang onto the bed, I could

smell the musky scent of his _____. But just
NOUN

as his hand touched my _____, his dog
BODY PART

pushed its way into the room, _____ and
VERB ENDING IN -ING

_____, and completely killing the mood.
VERB ENDING IN -ING

MUSICAL INTERLUDE
Fill in the Spank:

Song Title: _____

Musical Artist: _____

Instrument: _____

Number: _____

Room: _____

Piece of Clothing: _____

Verb Ending in -ING: _____

Event: _____

Accessory: _____

Relative: _____

Beverage: _____

Song Title: _____

Body Part (plural): _____

Pet Name: _____

Object: _____

Body Part: _____

I let him know I was in the mood by turning on

_____. It was a cover version,
SONG TITLE

by _____, and the long
MUSICAL ARTIST

_____ solo made it extra seductive. It only took
INSTRUMENT

him _____ minute(s) to come to the _____ once he
NUMBER   ROOM

heard the music. I was waiting for him in my _____,
PIECE OF CLOTHING

and nothing else. He started humming and _____.
VERB ENDING IN -ING

"Do you remember when this played at our _____?"
EVENT

I asked. He nodded, removing his _____. "And when
ACCESSORY

your _____ had too much _____ and
RELATIVE   BEVERAGE

they started singing _____?" By now, he
SONG TITLE

was ready to go. I jumped on the bed and threw my

_____ in the air. "Sing for me,
BODY PART (PLURAL)

_____," I panted. He reached behind him and
PET NAME

grabbed a(n) _____, which he used like
OBJECT

a mic. And then, when he was done singing, he used it

on my _____.
BODY PART

LONG DISTANCE CHARGES
Fill in the Spank:

Adjective: _____

US State: _____

Nickname: _____

Body Part: _____

Adjective: _____

Body Part: _____

Adjective: _____

Celebrity Name: _____

Piece of Furniture: _____

Body Part: _____

Body Part: _____

Profession: _____

Noun: _____

Year: _____

Number: _____

Number: _____

"Hello," she said. Her voice sounded sultry and _____.

ADJECTIVE

"This is _____. What's your name, sugar?"

US STATE

"Just call me _____," I told her. "Even over the

NICKNAME

phone, I can tell how sexy you are, baby. What do you look

like?" she asked. "Well, my _____ is

BODY PART

_____, and my _____ is

ADJECTIVE   BODY PART

_____," I said. "I like the sound of that.

ADJECTIVE

And I look like _____," she said. I sat

CELEBRITY NAME

back on my _____ and started rubbing my

PIECE OF FURNITURE

_____. "Oh yeah, I like that." "I'm kissing you.

BODY PART

And now my teeth have grabbed your _____,"

BODY PART

she said. I moaned with pleasure. "Are you really a

_____?" I asked. "Of course. I got my

PROFESSION

degree from _____ Spank University." "When

NOUN

did you graduate?" I asked, still rubbing furiously. "_____," she

YEAR

said. I could only moan again in response. "I'm sorry baby, that'll

be another _____ dollar(s) for the next _____ minute(s)." "I

NUMBER   NUMBER

accept the charges," I said.

TECH SAVVY
Fill in the Spank:

Direction: _____

Famous Location: _____

Noun: _____

Sound: _____

Body Part: _____

Adjective: _____

Emoji: _____

Time in the Future: _____

Celebrity: _____

Piece of Food: _____

Number: _____

Body Part: _____

Body Part: _____

Sexy Exclamation: _____

Adjective: _____

I had to swipe _____ when I saw his first profile
                    DIRECTION

picture, posing in front of the _____ with
                                    FAMOUS LOCATION

a _____. We matched right away, and a minute later,
        NOUN

I heard a _____ from my phone. He'd sent a picture
            SOUND

of his _____ with the note "Bet you never
                BODY PART

seen one like this before." I hadn't: it was _____. I sent
                                                ADJECTIVE

the _____ emoji, flirting back. "What are you doing
        EMOJI

_____?" he asked. "You," I
        TIME IN THE FUTURE

said. I sent him a GIF of _____ eating a(n)
                            CELEBRITY

_____. He texted, "Can I get a preview?"
        PIECE OF FOOD

I sent him a series of _____ picture(s), starting with
                        NUMBER

my _____ and ending with my bare _____.
        BODY PART   BODY PART

He texted back, "_____. You
                        SEXY EXCLAMATION

look _____!"
        ADJECTIVE

HEAVY HITTER
Fill in the Spank:

Object: _____

Body Part: _____

Color: _____

Number: _____

Adverb: _____

Noun (plural): _____

Noun (plural): _____

Profession: _____

Fictional Character: _____

Noun: _____

Body Part: _____

Number: _____

Silly Sound: _____

I couldn't tell if she was kidding when she held

out the _____ and said "Hit me with it. Hit me
             OBJECT

right in the _____." I looked into
                    BODY PART

her _____ eyes, and I could tell she was serious. I took
       COLOR

it from her hands—it must have weighed_____ pound(s).
                                          NUMBER

"Won't this hurt?" I said _____. We had used props
                                ADVERB

before, like _____ and _____, but
              NOUN (PLURAL)   NOUN (PLURAL)

this was different. "That's the point," she said. She reminded me

of a sexy _____ in that moment. It didn't
                  PROFESSION

hurt that she had dressed for the occasion by wearing

a _____costume. "Okay," I said, "Turn around
     FICTIONAL CHARACTER

and show me your _____." "What's my punishment?"
                        NOUN

she asked. Her _____trembled eagerly. "Oh, I
                      BODY PART

think about _____ strike(s) will do the trick." When the
               NUMBER

first strike landed, she let out a(n) _____.
                                            SILLY SOUND

"Again!" she cried, and I raised my hand.

LOOK-ALIKES
Fill in the Spank:

Famous Person: _____

Famous Person: _____

Famous Person: _____

Sexy Adjective: _____

Adjective: _____

Number: _____

Adjective: _____

Noun: _____

Famous Person: _____

Food: _____

Movie: _____

Sexy Verb: _____

Verb: _____

"You know who you look like?" she said. "_____."
                                                                  FAMOUS PERSON

I was flattered. I'd been told before that I looked like

_____, and even a little bit like
          FAMOUS PERSON

_____, but this was a new one. She
          FAMOUS PERSON

was stirring her coffee in that _____ way that
                                              SEXY ADJECTIVE

suggested she was _____. We'd been flirting
                                ADJECTIVE

for _____ hour(s), and I knew it was time to make my move.
      NUMBER

I pulled my computer closer to hers and opened a website

called _____ _____ Porno. "Well
              ADJECTIVE   NOUN

you look like _____. Want to see their
                        FAMOUS PERSON

sex tape?" Her eyes grew wide and she took a bite of her

_____. "I didn't know they had a sex tape! Is it
        FOOD

anything like _____?" "Sort
                              MOVIE

of," I said, "if you mean the acting is bad. At the end, they don't

even _____, they just _____ a
          SEXY VERB   VERB

lot in a bathtub."

- 13 -

TALK DIRTY TO ME
Fill in the Spank:

Piece of Furniture: _____

Number: _____

Something You Would Say to a Pet: _____

Body Part: _____

Something You Would Say to a Piece of Roast Beef: _____

Adjective: _____

Something You Would Say to a Construction Worker: _____

Body Part: _____

Something You Would Do to a Pig: _____

Term of Endearment: _____

Action: _____

Noun: _____

Action: _____

Noun: _____

Compliment: _____

She lay beside me on the _____, her eyes just _____
PIECE OF FURNITURE   NUMBER

inch(es) from mine. She grabbed my face and kissed me roughly.

"_____," she said.
SOMETHING YOU WOULD SAY TO A PET

"Ohhh," I replied, "are we talking dirty now?" She kissed me

again and slipped her hand down to my _____.
BODY PART

"_____," she said. Her
SOMETHING YOU WOULD SAY TO A PIECE OF ROAST BEEF

words immediately made me _____. "Oh yeah? Well,
ADJECTIVE

_____," I whispered.
SOMETHING YOU WOULD SAY TO A CONSTRUCTION WORKER

She shivered and bit her lip. "I love doing this with you."

Her fingers clenched around my _____. "I want
BODY PART

to _____," she said, looking
SOMETHING YOU WOULD DO TO A PIG

down. I flinched. "Maybe another day, my _____."
TERM OF ENDEARMENT

"Okay, then tell me what you want," she said, kissing

my earlobe. "I want you to _____ my
ACTION

_____." "Okay, and I want you to
NOUN

_____ my
ACTION

_____," she said.
NOUN

"_____," I said.
COMPLIMENT

– 15 –

NOW IT'S PERSONAL
Fill in the Spank:

Something You Wear (plural): _____

Liquid: _____

Body Part: _____

Name of Someone You Know: _____

Sport: _____

Adjective: _____

Name of a Friend: _____

Number: _____

Verb: _____

Body Part: _____

Name of Someone from Your Past: _____

Adjective: _____

Name of Someone You Went to High School with: _____

Number: _____

We were lying together in bed, wearing only our

_____, and sharing a cup
SOMETHING YOU WEAR (PLURAL)

of _____, when he asked me, "Did
LIQUID

you have a crush on me when we first met?" "No," I admitted,

trailing my fingers down his _____. "Actually, at
BODY PART

the time, I had a crush on _____.
NAME OF SOMEONE YOU KNOW

We used to play _____ together, and I thought they were
SPORT

so _____." "I thought you were sleeping
ADJECTIVE

with _____ at the time?" he said. "They weren't
NAME OF A FRIEND

any good," I said. "It only lasted _____week(s). They didn't
NUMBER

know how to _____." He kissed my
VERB

_____ and draped his arm over my stomach.
BODY PART

"Who was your first crush?" he asked. "I was totally in love with

_____. They always looked
NAME OF SOMEONE FROM YOUR PAST

so _____. Oh, and of course I had that whole school
ADJECTIVE

crush thing on _____." He
NAME OF SOMEONE YOU WENT TO HIGH SCHOOL WITH

sat up. "Wow, how many of our friends have you had a crush on?"

"_____," I said, "but you're my favorite."
NUMBER

FREE TO FETISHIZE
Fill in the spank:

Noise: _____

Emotion (adjective): _____

Number: _____

Movie Title: _____

Actor from That Movie: _____

Body Part: _____

Body Part: _____

Verb: _____

Noun: _____

Noun: _____

Room: _____

Adjective: _____

Body Part: _____

"_____," she sang out as she climaxed. She fell
        NOISE

back, exhausted and _____. He climbed off of
                    EMOTION (ADJECTIVE)

her, but she could see he was still aroused. She looked around his

room for clues about this man she had only met _____ day(s)
                                                 NUMBER

ago. She saw a poster on his wall for _____.
                                        MOVIE TITLE

He clearly had a crush on _____.
                            ACTOR FROM THAT MOVIE

"You didn't finish," she said. "Was it because I hit your

_____with my
            BODY PART

_____?" "No," he laughed.
            BODY PART

"It's just that sometimes I need a little extra . . . something. To

_____ my _____, if you know
      VERB   NOUN

what I mean." "I really don't know what you mean." He looked

at her solemnly. "Truth is, I have a _____ fetish."
                                          NOUN

She sat up, intrigued. "Really? And do you have one here?"

Eager, he said, "I keep one in my _____. The sight of it
                                        ROOM

makes me _____." She hesitated, but then
              ADJECTIVE

she looked down at her own _____.
                                    BODY PART

"I'll try anything once," she said.

– 19 –

THE EXHIBITIONISTS
Fill in the Spank:

Food: _____

Beverage: _____

City: _____

Noun (plural): _____

Adjective: _____

Noun (plural): _____

Location: _____

Animal (plural): _____

Verb: _____

Emotion (adjective): _____

Piece of Clothing: _____

Body Part: _____

Body Part You Can Open: _____

Exclamation: _____

Verb Ending in -ING: _____

She met him at their seats, way up in the stands, carrying a

jumbo _____ and a glass of
                FOOD

_____. It was their favorite team, the
        BEVERAGE

_____   _____ against
            CITY   NOUN (PLURAL)

the _____   _____ from
        ADJECTIVE   NOUN (PLURAL)

_____. It had rained like cats and
        LOCATION

_____ earlier, and the stands were
        ANIMAL (PLURAL)

nearly empty.   He looked around. "I've got the seventh-

inning itch," he said. "Ever want to _____ in
                                            VERB

public? "Is that a euphemism?" she asked. But she felt

_____. She climbed up on his lap,
        EMOTION (ADJECTIVE)

and he reached under her _____,
                                PIECE OF CLOTHING

inserting his _____ into her
                        BODY PART

_____. Nobody seemed to notice, so
        BODY PART YOU CAN OPEN

she began to bounce up and down. Then, someone sitting

behind them yelled, "_____!
                                EXCLAMATION

Are you two _____?!" "Is that
                    VERB ENDING IN -ING

a euphemism?" he said.

DOUBLE ENTENDRE
Fill in the Spank:

Verb: _____

Noun: _____

Body Part: _____

Verb: _____

Noun: _____

Article of Clothing: _____

Animal: _____

Adjective: _____

Verb: _____

Noun: _____

Something You Would Do to a Cow: _____

Sexy Noun: _____

"I want you to _____ my _____,
VERB   NOUN

if you know what I mean," she said, licking her

_____ seductively. "Well," I replied, "I'll do
BODY PART

that if you _____ my _____,
VERB   NOUN

if you get what I'm saying." She took off her

_____ and threw it at my face. "When I
ARTICLE OF CLOTHING

lie on this bed, I want you to act like a(n) _____, and
ANIMAL

get licking, if you get my meaning." "Oh, I understand loud

and _____. But when I'm down there, I hope
ADJECTIVE

you'll _____ my _____,
VERB   NOUN

if you get my drift?" She spread her legs wide and pointed down.

"_____," she commanded.
SOMETHING YOU WOULD DO TO A COW

"Well, you know what they say," I said. "One in the hand is worth

two in the _____."
SEXY NOUN

SONNETS AND SNOGS
Fill in the Spank:

Emotion (adjective): _____

Noun: _____

Body Part: _____

Author: _____

Body Part: _____

Color: _____

Sexy Verb: _____

Organ: _____

Body Part: _____

Number: _____

Body Part: _____

Verb Ending in -ING: _____

Author: _____

He held a piece of paper in his hand, obviously feeling

_____. "I wrote it for you," he said. We were
EMOTION (ADJECTIVE)

sitting together under the shade of a(n) _____, with
NOUN

his hand resting on my _____. "It's a sonnet,"
BODY PART

he said. "Like the ones _____ used to write."
AUTHOR

He shifted his _____ and began to read:
BODY PART

Roses are _____, violets are blue,
COLOR

I want to _____, and to do it with you,
SEXY VERB

The _____ inside me beats like a drum,
ORGAN

I'll lick your _____, until you come.
BODY PART

"I thought sonnets were supposed to be _____ line(s)."
NUMBER

He leaned in and kissed me, his hand moving up

my _____. Between kisses, he breathed, "I'm not
BODY PART

very good at poetry. But I'm great at _____." I
VERB ENDING IN -ING

laughed as his breath tickled my neck. "Okay, but for

future reference, I think _____ is really sexy."
AUTHOR

ARTISTIC INTENTIONS
Fill in the Spank:

Piece of Furniture: _____

Body Part: _____

Something You Wear: _____

Noun: _____

Noun: _____

Verb: _____

Object: _____

Profession: _____

Verb (past tense): _____

Body Part: _____

Verb (past tense): _____

Noun: _____

Sexy Noun: _____

Body Part: _____

Famous Artist: _____

Adjective: _____

I found her lying on the _____ with

her_____ completely exposed. She was

wearing a_____ on her head, and the way the

light hit her, she looked like a _____ from an old

English painting. I was captivated by her _____,

fixated on it. "Model for me," I said. "I want to watch you

_____." She covered her face with her

_____, embarrassed. "I couldn't possibly," she

said, "I'm not a _____." But even as she

said it, she stood and _____. I

regarded her with the _____ of an

artist, my lust growing each time she _____.

She danced over to the _____, and picked up

her _____. "Where do you want me to stick

this?" she asked. "How about in my _____?" I'm

no _____, but I thought that sounded like

a(n)_____ idea.

ALL TIED UP
Fill in the Spank:

Something You Sit on: _____

Body Part (plural): _____

Material: _____

Adjective: _____

Pet Name: _____

Verb: _____

Adjective: _____

Body Part: _____

Body Part You Open: _____

Adjective: _____

Verb: _____

Something You Tie: _____

He pointed to the _____. "Sit," he commanded. I
                    SOMETHING YOU SIT ON

did as I was told. The collar around my neck was a symbol of my

devotion to him. "Put your _____ in the air," he said.
                          BODY PART (PLURAL)

I obliged. He grabbed a length of rope from the table. It was made

of _____, and it looked _____.
        MATERIAL   ADJECTIVE

"Will you—" I started to speak, but he cut me off.

"Silence, _____!" he snapped. "Who said you
                PET NAME

could _____?" I held still as he tied my
            VERB

wrists. The rope on my skin felt_____.
                                        ADJECTIVE

My privates began to feel warm as I imagined his

_____ in my _____,
        BODY PART   BODY PART YOU OPEN

his cold, _____eyes staring at me. And
              ADJECTIVE

me, unable to move or even _____.
                                    VERB

Totally powerless. I shuddered as he then took a

_____, and wrapped it around
        SOMETHING YOU TIE

my neck. "Good pet," he said.

FURRY AND FURRIER
Fill in the Spank:

Animal (plural): _____

Animal (plural): _____

Animal (plural): _____

Cartoon Character: _____

Cartoon Character: _____

Noun: _____

Noun: _____

Drink: _____

Fabric/Material: _____

Body Part: _____

Adjective: _____

Adjective: _____

The furry convention was in full swing by the time I even noticed

them. All around me were _____ and
                                                ANIMAL (PLURAL)

_____, and even some
            ANIMAL   (PLURAL)

_____. There were people dressed up
        ANIMAL (PLURAL)

like _____ and _____,
        CARTOON CHARACTER   CARTOON CHARACTER

which I found particularly sexy. But then I noticed them.

They were wearing a _____ costume. I had never
                                NOUN

seen anything like it. I myself was dressed like the sexiest thing I

could think of: a(n) _____. I walked up to
                                NOUN

them and offered a glass of _____.
                                                    DRINK

"I appreciate that you've used _____ to
                                        FABRIC/MATERIAL

make your costume. It must feel nice against your

_____." They nodded their oversized head.
        BODY PART

"How would you feel about making this a party of two?"

they said. I started feeling _____, even under
                                        ADJECTIVE

my _____ furry suit. "Your room or mine?"
            ADJECTIVE

I said.

STRIP PLEASE
Fill in the Spank:

Adjective: _____

Noun (plural): _____

Name of Your First Pet: _____

Street You Grew Up on: _____

Song Title: _____

Verb: _____

Song Title: _____

Man's Name: _____

Number: _____

Piece of Clothing: _____

Store: _____

Body Part: _____

Piece of Clothing: _____

Body Part: _____

Number: _____

The name of the club was _____ _____,
                                      ADJECTIVE   NOUN (PLURAL)

and it catered to the high-class clientele. _____
                                 NAME OF YOUR FIRST PET

_____ was their most popular dancer. She
STREET YOU GREW UP ON

could do anything on a pole. Her favorite song to dance to

was _____, and she would grind and shimmy
           SONG TITLE

and _____ like the best of them. One
           VERB

day, _____ started playing, and she began to dance,
     SONG TITLE

catching the attention of _____. He was new at the
                 MAN'S NAME

club, _____ years old, wearing a _____ that
      NUMBER   PIECE OF CLOTHING

he'd bought at _____. He looked expensive.
          STORE

She dipped down and shook her _____ right in
               BODY PART

his face. Then she removed her _____,
               PIECE OF CLOTHING

and he felt himself getting turned on. He could see her

_____, and he wanted to touch it.
BODY PART

He held up a _____ dollar bill. "For you," he said. "If you
       NUMBER

come closer."

BANG, MARRY, KILL
Fill in the Spank:

Trendy Noun: _____

Profession: _____

Silly Word: _____

Name of a Friend: _____

Name of a Coworker: _____

Name of a Friend: _____

Location: _____

Room: _____

Foreplay Activity (verb): _____

Sound: _____

Sexual Activity (verb): _____

Sexual Activity (verb): _____

Location: _____

Emotion (adjective): _____

Profession: _____

"Okay," she said, reading from her magazine. "According to this

magical prediction quiz in _____ Magazine, Psychic
                                    TRENDY NOUN

Mistress and _____ Madame _____ says
                  PROFESSION   SILLY WORD

you're going to bang _____, marry
                              NAME OF A FRIEND

_____, and kill _____.
    NAME OF A COWORKER   NAME OF A FRIEND

"What?!" I cried, ripping the magazine from her hands. "It can't

be!" She took the magazine and kept reading. "It says when you

two bang, you're going to meet up at a _____,
                                                LOCATION

and then make your way to the _____, where
                                            ROOM

they will _____ until you start moaning
            FOREPLAY ACTIVITY (VERB)

and making _____ noises. Then you'll
                        SOUND

_____ and _____ at
    SEXUAL ACTIVITY (VERB)   SEXUAL ACTIVITY (VERB)

the same time, which will give you a nosebleed. When they take

you to the _____ to get your nose checked out,
                  LOCATION

they'll feel so turned on and _____, they'll start to
                                    EMOTION (ADJECTIVE)

kiss you right there in front of the _____."
                                            PROFESSION

"It can't say all that!" I said. She smirked behind the magazine.

"Never doubt a psychic guru," she said.

PICKUP ARTIST
Fill in the Spank:

Alcoholic Beverage: _____

Body Part: _____

Body Part: _____

Location: _____

Verb Ending in -ING: _____

Food Item: _____

Something Wet: _____

US State: _____

Body Part (plural): _____

Exclamation: _____

When the bartender placed a(n) _____ in front of me,
ALCOHOLIC BEVERAGE

I had a feeling it was the man at the end of the bar who had ordered

it. He came over, and I felt his breath tickling my _____.
BODY PART

"If I said you had a beautiful _____, would you hold it
BODY PART

against me?" he said. I rolled my eyes and took a drink. "No?

Well God must be missing an angel, because you're clearly

from _____." When I didn't respond, he sat next to
LOCATION

me and flashed a smile. "You must be tired from _____
VERB ENDING IN -ING

through my mind all night." I glared at him. "You're the literal

worst." He simply smiled and said, "Are you made of _____?
FOOD ITEM

'Cause you look sweet as pie. I hope you have a(n) _____,
SOMETHING WET

because you're on FIRE!" No free drink was worth this, so I

started to stand up. "Wait!" he said, "Are you from _____?
US STATE

Because you're the only Ten I See. It would help if I had a map,

see, because I got lost in your _____." I paused
BODY PART (PLURAL)

before I walked away. "You know, I've lost my phone number,"

I said. "Do you think I could have yours?" His eyes lit up.

"_____! Really?!" "No," I said.
EXCLAMATION!

DRESSING UP FOR THE EVENING
Fill in the Spank:

Adjective: _____

Type of Art:_____

Type of Person (plural): _____

Composer: _____

Sensation: _____

Body Part: _____

Exclamation: _____

Emotion (adjective): _____

Adjective: _____

Adjective: _____

Body Part: _____

Line from a Song: _____

Noise: _____

Sound You'd Make When Startled:_____

Number: _____

He'd worn a tuxedo. She'd worn a ball gown. They'd both worn

vibrating underwear. Tonight was going to be _____.
                                                ADJECTIVE

They were going to the opera: _____ of
                                      TYPE OF ART

the _____, by _____. They each
      TYPE OF PERSON (PLURAL)   COMPOSER

had a remote for the other's vibrating underwear. Sometime during

the first act, he felt a _____ around his _____,
                          SENSATION   BODY PART

and wondered if she'd turned it on. Then, his pants

began to buzz. "_____!" he cried out. The
                      EXCLAMATION

people around them were clearly _____ with
                                    EMOTION (ADJECTIVE)

the outburst. They shushed him and turned back around. His

groin felt _____ and_____. She was evil
              ADJECTIVE   ADJECTIVE

for turning it up so high all at once, but he couldn't deny the

lust forming around his _____. The soprano sang
                              BODY PART

"_____," and then there was
              LINE FROM A SONG

another _____from his pants.
                      NOISE

"_____!" His pants were going to be wet
      SOUND YOU'D MAKE WHEN STARTLED

by the end of the _____-hour opera, he just knew it.
                      NUMBER

TOY CHEST
Fill in the Spank:

Adjective: _____

Noun (plural): _____

Type of Material: _____

Number: _____

Noun (plural): _____

Body Part (plural): _____

Celebrity: _____

Object: _____

Body Part: _____

Emotion (adjective): _____

Sex Toy: _____

I couldn't believe my eyes when I saw his toy chest. It was enormous,

and full of every type of _____ instrument you could
                                 ADJECTIVE

think of. Dildos the size of _____, whips made
                              NOUN (PLURAL)

of _____, vibrators meant to be used
   TYPE OF MATERIAL

by _____ people simultaneously. There were different
   NUMBER

types of rope, anal plugs shaped like _____, and
                                        NOUN (PLURAL)

fleshy synthetic _____, made from actual casts
                 BODY PART (PLURAL)

of _____'s body. I picked up a dildo shaped
   CELEBRITY

like a(n) _____ and rubbed it against his
          OBJECT

_____. He squirmed in anticipation. "I
BODY PART

hope my toys don't make you feel _____,"
                                  EMOTION (ADJECTIVE)

he said. "Not if you let me use this on you," I said, holding up a

_____. "Anything but that!" he said. "I'm
SEX TOY

still sore."

FIRST DATE
Fill in the Spank:

Beverage: _____

Woman's Name: _____

Exclamation: _____

Type of Residence: _____

Sexy Noun: _____

Something You Would Wear: _____

Sexual Activity (verb): _____

Sexy Noun: _____

Sexual Activity (verb): _____

Body Part: _____

Noun: _____

Type of Clothing: _____

Their plates were clean, and they'd already finished a

whole bottle of _____. She looked at her date,
                    BEVERAGE

_____, and whispered, "My place is just
         WOMAN'S NAME

around the corner." Her date's eyebrows shot up.

"_____. You're awfully confident,
         EXCLAMATION

aren't you?" But she laughed and added, "And what would

we do at your_____?"
                    TYPE OF RESIDENCE

"I have a(n) _____ at home," she said. She
                 SEXY NOUN

pulled the top of her dress down, "And I'm wearing

a(n) _____ under this. Maybe we could go
      SOMETHING YOU WOULD WEAR

back and I could show you how to _____ with
                                    SEXUAL ACTIVITY (VERB)

a(n) _____." Her date leaned closer. "And what
      SEXY NOUN

makes you think I'll do all of this on a first date?" She smiled.

"Because all night, your eyes have been telling me that you want to

_____. And because you've been staring
    SEXUAL ACTIVITY (VERB)

at my _____ for hours." Her date grabbed her
          BODY PART

hand. "Well that's because you're as sexy as a(n) _____ in
                                                      NOUN

a(n) _____."
      TYPE OF CLOTHING

HALLOWEEN IS FOR HUSSIES
Fill in the Spank:

Time on the Clock: _____

Noun: _____

Article of Clothing: _____

Something You Would Say to a Captive: _____

Fictional Character: _____

Something You Would Wear: _____

Body Part (plural): _____

Material: _____

Fabric: _____

Halloween Decoration (plural): _____

Type of Candy (plural): _____

Euphemism for Having Sex (past tense): _____

Halloween Adjective: _____

"C'mon we're gonna be late!" I called. It was already

_____, and we had a Halloween party to get to.
TIME ON THE CLOCK

She came down the stairs and I drew in a breath: she was dressed

like a sexy _____. I didn't know she owned such a
NOUN

short _____. By the time she got to the bottom
ARTICLE OF CLOTHING

of the steps, all thoughts of the party were gone. I pushed her

up against the bannister. " _____,"
SOMETHING YOU WOULD SAY TO A CAPTIVE

I growled. I was dressed like _____, and
FICTIONAL CHARACTER

I felt the spirit of the character filling me as I unbuckled

my _____. She kissed me, and
SOMETHING YOU WOULD WEAR

our _____ pressed together, restrained
BODY PART (PLURAL)

only by the tight _____ and _____ that
MATERIAL   FABRIC

made up our costumes. Our bodies crashed against the hall table,

and _____ and _____ flew
HALLOWEEN DECORATION (PLURAL)   TYPE OF CANDY (PLURAL)

everywhere. Mini candies littered the ground at our feet, as we

passionately _____, hoping nobody
EUPHEMISM FOR HAVING SEX (PAST TENSE)

would ring our doorbell and ruin the _____ mood.
HALLOWEEN ADJECTIVE

HOME FOR THE HOLIDAYS
Fill in the spank:

Relative: _____

Something You'd Say at Christmas: _____

Number: _____

Noun (plural): _____

Clothing Size: _____

Something Associated with Christmas: _____

Something an Elf Would Say: _____

Food Item (plural): _____

Something Bad: _____

Body Part: _____

Something Santa Would Say: _____

Someone You Know: _____

Body Part: _____

We had to be quiet. After all, my _____ was sleeping
_____RELATIVE

in the next room over. I didn't want them thinking Santa had

come early. Pun intended. "_____," I
_____SOMETHING YOU'D SAY AT CHRISTMAS

whispered in her ear. We were in my old room, where I'd slept

when I was only _____ years old. The sheets still had cartoon
_____NUMBER

_____ all over them. "Do you want me in a stocking?"
NOUN (PLURAL)

I said, holding up a _____ condom. She purred "Yes" in
_____CLOTHING SIZE

response. "I'll be a(n) _____, and you
_____SOMETHING ASSOCIATED WITH CHRISTMAS

be an elf," I said. She crawled down my body, opened her mouth,

looked up, and said, "_____."
_____SOMETHING AN ELF WOULD SAY

Christmas nearly arrived right then and there. "Be careful," I

warned, "Or you'll be eating my milk and _____early."
_____FOOD ITEM (PLURAL)

"Sounds tempting," she said, her mouth already full. "Were you

naughty this year?" "I was as bad as _____," I moaned.
_____SOMETHING BAD

She licked my _____. "What would Santa say?" "He'd say
_____BODY PART

'_____.'" I leaned back and tried not to think
___SOMETHING SANTA WOULD SAY

of _____ sleeping in the next room. It was
_____SOMEONE YOU KNOW

so hard to stay quiet with her _____ on my sack of goodies.
_____BODY PART

– 47 –

MY FAVORITE PET
Fill in the Spank:

Woman's Name: _____

Article of Clothing: _____

Body Part (plural): _____

Man's Name: _____

Cartoon Character: _____

Sex Toy: _____

Animal: _____

Something You Would Say to a Pet: _____

Body Part: _____

Sexy Verb: _____

Body Part: _____

Sex Toy: _____

Something You Would Order Your Partner to Do: _____

Something You Would Yell in Traffic: _____

_____ wore a black leather _____ and
    WOMAN'S NAME   **ARTICLE OF CLOTHING**

a corset that accentuated her _____. At her feet
                                     BODY PART (PLURAL)

sat _____, her favorite submissive pet. He wore a collar
       MAN'S NAME

that had his chosen name engraved on it: _____.
                                      CARTOON CHARACTER

He was obediently waiting for instructions. She snapped

her _____ across his back. "Today," she commanded,
       SEX TOY

"you are my _____. Get on all fours!" He immediately did
           ANIMAL

as she asked. "_____," she cooed. He could
           SOMETHING YOU WOULD SAY TO A PET

feel his mouth salivating, and his _____ hardening
                              BODY PART

at her words. He would do anything for his Mistress—even

_____. "Now kiss my _____," she said
     SEXY VERB   **BODY PART**

harshly. He complied immediately, and she ran the tip of

her _____ across his shoulder. He shuddered.
       SEX TOY

"_____," she said. He looked
    SOMETHING YOU WOULD ORDER YOUR PARTNER TO DO

up at her with wide eyes, but didn't move fast enough for her

liking. She grabbed his hair. "_____!"
                                    SOMETHING YOU WOULD YELL IN TRAFFIC

she shouted. He jumped at her words, never wanting to displease

his Mistress.

RIGHT TO REMAIN SILENT
Fill in the Spank:

Crime: _____

Adjective: _____

Body Part (plural): _____

Adjective: _____

Crime: _____

Crime: _____

Something You Would Call a Sexy Man: _____

Body Part: _____

Something a Criminal Would Say: _____

Object (plural): _____

Sexy Nickname: _____

I made sure the handcuffs were nice and tight. I'd arrested

him for _____, but as I watched his
                    CRIME

_____ face, smiling for his mug shots, I knew I
        ADJECTIVE

would have to interrogate him myself. In the interrogation room,

I leaned over so he could see my _____.
                                        BODY PART (PLURAL)

"You have the right to remain _____," I said. I ran
                                      ADJECTIVE

my hands over his wrists. "Anything you want held against

you?" He had three priors: one for _____,
                                                CRIME

one for _____, and one for being a
                  CRIME

_____. I unbuckled my belt.
      SOMETHING YOU WOULD CALL A SEXY MAN

"We'll be taking you uptown," I said, looking down at my

_____. "Unless you want to go downtown?"
      BODY PART

"_____," he said,
            SOMETHING A CRIMINAL WOULD SAY

but I could see him staring at my fine _____.
                                                OBJECT (PLURAL)

He held up his bound wrists and leaned toward me. "Book me,

Officer _____."
                SEXY NICKNAME

– 51 –

HONEYMOON HOTEL
Fill in the Spank:

Man's Name: _____

Fictional Character: _____

Location: _____

Type of Outfit: _____

Something You Would Wear: _____

Adjective: _____

Something That Turns You On: _____

Body Part: _____

Something You Would Wear: _____

Sexual Activity (Verb): _____

Something Your Fictional Character Would Say: _____

Term of Endearment: _____

"_____," she said, "it's our honeymoon! Do you

really have to dress up like _____ today? Isn't

it enough that we're finally in _____, the place you've

always wanted to go?" She sighed and pulled the covers down.

"And look," she said, "I'm wearing a(n) _____.

Isn't this sexy enough for you?" He jumped onto the bed next to

her and removed his _____. "You

look _____," he said, kissing her deeply.

"But you knew when you married me that this is like

_____ to me—it gets me hot."

She caressed his _____ and kissed him back.

"I did know," she said, "And I love you." She ripped off

his _____ and grabbed him around the

waist. "And you knew when you married ME that you'd need to

_____. A lot." He dove under the covers and started

kissing her body. "_____!"

she heard him say from under the blankets. She laughed. "Happy

honeymoon, _____."

WORK IT OUT
Fill in the Spank:

Number: _____

Body Part: _____

Something You Would Say in a Strenuous Situation: _____

Sound: _____

Article of Clothing: _____

Adjective: _____

Exclamation of Disgust: _____

Piece of Furniture: _____

Sexy Verb Ending in -ING: _____

Number: _____

Exclamation of Rage: _____

Adjective: _____

Name of a Podcast: _____

I could feel her eyes on me as I lifted the _____-pound dumbbell.
NUMBER

Sweat dripped down her _____, and I wished I could
BODY PART

taste it. I decided to show off a little by dead lifting the barbell

next to me. "_____!"
SOMETHING YOU WOULD SAY IN A STRENUOUS SITUATION

I grunted. I let the heavy bar fall to the ground with a

_____. She smiled at me and seductively lifted her arms
SOUND

above her head, stretching. Her tight _____ strained
ARTICLE OF CLOTHING

around her taut, _____ form. I picked up the barbell
ADJECTIVE

again. "_____!" I screamed as I lifted it. I
EXCLAMATION OF DISGUST

decided it was too much weight. I should wait to break my

back with her, on a _____, burning calories
PIECE OF FURNITURE

and _____. I just needed to get her to talk to
SEXY VERB ENDING IN -ING

me. I grabbed the _____-pound dumbbells this time for some
NUMBER

bicep curls. "_____," I shouted as I
EXCLAMATION OF RAGE

lifted the heavy weight. Finally, she walked over and caught

my eye. She pursed her beautiful, _____ lips and
ADJECTIVE

said: "Excuse me, could you keep it down? Some of us are trying

to listen to _____."
NAME OF A PODCAST

SWEET SPOT
Fill in the Spank:

Place You Would Go for Fun: _____

Instrument: _____

Song Title: _____

Adjective: _____

Body Part: _____

Article of Clothing: _____

Noun: _____

Type of Facial Hair: _____

Something You Would Whisper: _____

Song Title: _____

Body Part: _____

Instrument: _____

I decided to go out to _____ on my own one

PLACE YOU WOULD GO FOR FUN

night. A band was playing, and I couldn't help but notice the dark-

haired _____ player, looking fine as hell as he

INSTRUMENT

sang back-up vocals to _____. After their spot, he

SONG TITLE

approached me at the bar, and before I knew it, we were making our

way through the _____ crowd toward the dark hallway at

ADJECTIVE

the back. In the shadows, he pushed me against the wall, and I felt

his _____, hard against my thigh. His hands slipped

BODY PART

up my _____, and I inhaled the musky

ARTICLE OF CLOTHING

scent of his cologne: _____, by Calvin Klein.

NOUN

He was tall, with long hair and a(n) _____.

TYPE OF FACIAL HAIR

His stubble scratched against my cheek as he whispered,

"_____." "Anyone might see

SOMETHING YOU WOULD WHISPER

us here," I said, but the musician didn't care. He

started humming _____ as he nipped and

SONG TITLE

grazed at my _____. "Let me play you like

BODY PART

a(n) _____," he said, "and they'll just

INSTRUMENT

think we're making beautiful music."

HEROES
Fill in the Spank:

Adjective: _____

Adjective: _____

Noun: _____

Adjective: _____

Noun: _____

Verb: _____

Body Part: _____

Food: _____

Number: _____

Piece of Clothing: _____

Adjective: _____

Liquid: _____

They met in a dark, _____ alleyway. "Hello again,
ADJECTIVE

_____ _____ Girl," he
ADJECTIVE NOUN

growled. "I'm _____ _____ Man. I
ADJECTIVE NOUN

couldn't help admiring how fast you can _____."
VERB

He ran his hand down her _____, seductively.
BODY PART

"What's your super power?" she asked. Her voice sounded

as sweet as _____. He put his hands on
FOOD

her waist. "I can grow to _____ times the size of a
NUMBER

normal man," he said. She looked down at his costume.

"Good thing I'm stretchy. Show me." He unbuckled his

_____, and she gasped.
PIECE OF CLOTHING

"It's _____!" she said. "You really do have
ADJECTIVE

super powers." He pressed her up against the brick wall of

the alleyway, and some _____ dripped down
LIQUID

on them from the fire escape above. "We really need to clean up

this city," he said.

READY, CAMERA, ACTION
Fill in the Spank:

Number: _____

Movie Director: _____

Adjective: _____

Adjective: _____

Noun (plural): _____

Famous Actor: _____

Movie-Related Profession: _____

Article of Clothing: _____

Sexual Verb Ending in -ING: _____

Body Part: _____

Color: _____

Something You Would Find on a Movie Set: _____

Famous Line from a Movie: _____

We'd been working together for _____ month(s) on the
NUMBER

set of the newest _____ blockbuster:
MOVIE DIRECTOR

" _____ and _____ _____."
ADJECTIVE   ADJECTIVE   NOUN (PLURAL)

The talent, _____, had gone for the day, and Mike,
FAMOUS ACTOR

the _____, turned the camera back on when
MOVIE-RELATED PROFESSION

we were alone. "Ever wanted to make your own movie?" he asked,

positioning himself in front of the camera. I rushed to his side,

dropping my _____ on the way. In no time,
ARTICLE OF CLOTHING

we were _____, and he had his hands
SEXUAL VERB ENDING IN -ING

all over my _____. The camera's little
BODY PART

_____ light
COLOR

told me we were recording. I decided to put on a show, leaning

against the _____ and
SOMETHING YOU WOULD FIND ON A MOVIE SET

screaming   out   whenever   Mike   touched   me:

" _____!"
FAMOUS LINE FROM A MOVIE

THE KAMA SUTRA
Fill in the Spank:

Number: _____

Euphemism for Having Sex: _____

Adjective: _____

Noun: _____

Body Part (plural): _____

Body Part: _____

Sexy Verb: _____

Something You Would Yell During Sex: _____

Adjective: _____

Noun: _____

Sexy Verb: _____

Sexy Verb: _____

Profession: _____

Exclamation: _____

Adjective: _____

He flipped to page _____ of the book we'd bought: *Secrets*
NUMBER

of the Kama Sutra: 64 Ways to _____.
EUPHEMISM FOR HAVING SEX

"Oooh, this one looks good!" he said. "It's called the

_____ _____,
ADJECTIVE   NOUN

and you wrap your _____ around my
BODY PART (PLURAL)

_____, and then we
BODY PART

_____. To heighten the sensation, you
SEXY VERB

can yell ' _____.'"
SOMETHING YOU WOULD YELL DURING SEX

I flipped the page over. "I don't know," I said, "I like the

sound of the _____ _____.
ADJECTIVE   NOUN

This is when you _____ and I
SEXY VERB

simultaneously _____, but I do it backwards
SEXY VERB

and upside down. I think it helps if you pretend to be a

_____." "_____!"
PROFESSION   EXCLAMATION

he said. "That sounds _____!"
ADJECTIVE

HARDLY HIKING
Fill in the Spank:

Number: _____

Type of Plant (plural): _____

Sex Toy: _____

Article of Clothing: _____

Object: _____

Type of Person (plural): _____

Type of Animal (plural): _____

Something You Would Read on a Sign: _____

Type of Underwear: _____

Body Part: _____

Adjective: _____

Expression: _____

Expletive: _____

Jonathon knew Harry wasn't much of a hiker, but he'd expected

to go at least _____ mile(s) before Harry needed a break.

NUMBER

Apparently, Harry was done hiking. He sat on a stump, even

though it was covered with _____. Then

TYPE OF PLANT (PLURAL)

he opened his backpack and drew out a _____ and

SEX TOY

a condom. "What are you doing?!" Jonathan said. "This is

what you packed for the hike?" Harry smiled and stripped off

his _____. "This and a(n) _____. Oh, and

ARTICLE OF CLOTHING   OBJECT

some lube." Jonathan watched as Harry opened the condom

wrapper. "But we could run into _____! Or

TYPE OF PERSON (PLURAL)

even _____!" Harry unbuckled his belt and

TYPE OF ANIMAL (PLURAL)

motioned toward a sign that said: _____.

SOMETHING YOU WOULD READ ON A SIGN

"Nobody will see us out here. Now where should we do it? There?"

He took off his _____ and sat on a patch of green

TYPE OF UNDERWEAR

plants. His _____ looked hard and _____ as

BODY PART   ADJECTIVE

he rubbed his body against the grass with a(n) _____ on

EXPRESSION

his face. "Wait," Jonathan said, pointing to the ground. "Isn't that

poison ivy?" Harry froze. "_____!"

EXPLETIVE

ROMEO AND JULIET
Fill in the Spank:

Something Soft (plural): _____

Time of Day: _____

Body Part: _____

Sexy Adjective: _____

Sexy Adjective: _____

Type of Person (plural): _____

Adverb: _____

Body Part: _____

Sexual Verb: _____

Body Part: _____

Romeo stared at his bride, nestled beside him in a bed

of _____. "Did my heart love till now? Forswear
    SOMETHING SOFT (PLURAL)

it, sight! For I ne'er saw true beauty till this _____."
                                                    TIME OF DAY

Juliet smiled and lifted the blanket, exposing her bare

_____. "These _____ delights have
    BODY PART   SEXY ADJECTIVE

_____ ends," she said. "My lips, two blushing
    SEXY ADJECTIVE

_____, ready stand to smooth that
    TYPE OF PERSON (PLURAL)

rough touch with a tender kiss." With that, Romeo leaned

down and kissed Juliet _____ on the _____.
                            ADVERB   BODY PART

"You kiss by the book," she said. When she laughed, he

kissed her again, this time more fervently. "Thus, with a kiss,

I _____," she moaned. Romeo leaned back and
    SEXUAL VERB

stroked his Juliet. "Are we not a pair of star-crossed lovers?"

Juliet wrapped her hand around his _____.
                                            BODY PART

"It is a good thing you woke up before I killed myself. Or this

story might have had a very different ending indeed."

PRIDE AND PREJUDICE
Fill in the Spank:

Noun: _____

Noun: _____

Man's Name: _____

Sexy Noun (plural): _____

Verb (past tense): _____

Body Part: _____

Thing That Makes Noise: _____

Verb: _____

Historical Noun: _____

Exclamation: _____

Color: _____

Body Part: _____

Personality Trait (noun): _____

Adjective: _____

It is a truth universally acknowledged, that a single man in

possession of a(n) _____, must be in want of
                                        NOUN

a(n) _____. So it was with Mr. Darcy, first name
                  NOUN

_____, who had amassed a great number of
        MAN'S NAME

_____ in his life, and now hoped to
    SEXY NOUN (PLURAL)

share them with Miss Elizabeth Bennet. As they

_____ around the garden, he could tell
        VERB (PAST TENSE)

Miss Bennet was flirting. She showed him only her

_____, but he could tell that she was
            BODY PART

lovely. When she said, "Do you like the sound of the

_____?" he heard in her tone a different
        THING THAT MAKES NOISE

question: "Do you want to _____ my _____?"
                                            VERB   HISTORICAL NOUN

When he was sure they were alone, he kissed her deeply.

"_____," she exclaimed. Her face turned _____.
    EXCLAMATION   COLOR

"I apologize for being so forward, Miss Bennet," said Mr. Darcy.

He took her _____ and placed a gentle kiss upon it.
                        BODY PART

"I could easily forgive your _____," she said,
                                        PERSONALITY TRAIT (NOUN)

"if I were not so _____, myself."
                                ADJECTIVE

HAPPILY EVER AFTER
Fill in the Spank:

Room: _____

City: _____

Something You Would Do to a Popsicle: _____

Sexual Activity (verb): _____

Animal: _____

Animal: _____

Article of Clothing: _____

Relative: _____

Sexual Activity (verb): _____

Adjective: _____

Noun: _____

Noun: _____

Sexy Adjective: _____

Body Part: _____

Time in the Future: _____

I knew one day my prince would come. I just didn't think that

would mean "in his hand," in the middle of the _____, in
                                                    ROOM

a castle in _____. I knew I was the fairest lady,
                 CITY

but still. He motioned to the nectar in his hand.

" _____," he suggested. I
        SOMETHING YOU WOULD DO TO A POPSICLE

frowned and shook my head. "That's okay," I said, "why don't we

_____instead?" Outside the window, my
        SEXUAL ACTIVITY (VERB)

_____ and _____ friends were looking on.
        ANIMAL   ANIMAL

"Shoo!" I said as my _____ dropped to the ground.
                            ARTICLE OF CLOTHING

My fairy _____ had given it to me, but I couldn't
              RELATIVE

_____ with all those ruffles. My
        SEXUAL ACTIVITY (VERB)

prince regarded me, a(n) _____ look
                                           ADJECTIVE

in his eye. "I wished upon a _____ that some day I would
                                      NOUN

find you, my little _____." "Shut up and kiss me," I said.
                            NOUN

Don't get me wrong, I liked a chivalrous prince as much as the

next pauper, but I was _____. "Do you think we'll be
                              SEXY ADJECTIVE

happy forever?" he asked. I grabbed his _____. "Oh,
                                                    BODY PART

I think at least until _____," I said.
                              TIME IN THE FUTURE

FLUFFERS
Fill in the Spank:

Porn Star Name: _____

Color of Your Underwear: _____

Last Sweet Thing You Ate: _____

Sexy Adjective: _____

Person's Name: _____

Color: _____

Body Part: _____

Something You Would Whisper: _____

Number: _____

Sexy Verb Ending in -ING: _____

Body Part: _____

Adjective: _____

Something a Volcano Would Do: _____

The director said, "Cut!" and Randy Thickbird's costar,

_____, left the set for a five-minute break. Randy
<small>PORN STAR NAME</small>

had to be ready, because his next costar, _____
<small>COLOR OF YOUR UNDERWEAR</small>

_____, was on the way. Between takes, he
<small>LAST SWEET THING YOU ATE</small>

would need to stay _____. That's why the fluffer
<small>SEXY ADJECTIVE</small>

came over. Their name was _____, and they had
<small>PERSON'S NAME</small>

deep _____ eyes. They ran their hands all over Randy's
<small>COLOR</small>

body, lingering on his _____. Their mouth kissed
<small>BODY PART</small>

up and down his neck, stopping at his ear to whisper,

"_____." Randy felt _____ eyes
<small>SOMETHING YOU WOULD WHISPER</small>   <small>NUMBER</small>

on him, as the whole production staff watched the

fluffer _____. Randy responded by leaning
<small>SEXY VERB ENDING IN -ING</small>

back and pinching his own _____ until he
<small>BODY PART</small>

felt _____. As the heat grew inside
<small>ADJECTIVE</small>

him, he realized the fluffer better stop, or he was going to

_____ before the cameras
<small>SOMETHING A VOLCANO WOULD DO</small>

were rolling.

THREE'S A CROWD
Fill in the Spank:

Noun: _____

Sexy Verb Ending in -ING: _____

Sexy Verb Ending in -ING: _____

Something You Would Wear: _____

Name of Person You Know: _____

Sound: _____

Something Hot: _____

Verb Ending in -ING: _____

Woman's Name: _____

Article of Clothing: _____

Something You Would Say in Bed: _____

Emotion (adjective): _____

Body Part: _____

I'd never had sex in a closet before, but then I'd never had sex at

a(n) _____-themed party before either. He was ready to
                NOUN

go by the time the door shut, _____ and
                                    SEXY VERB ENDING IN -ING

_____ before I even had time to get
    SEXY VERB ENDING IN -ING

my _____ off. He pinned me
        SOMETHING YOU WOULD WEAR

against the wall, whispering, "Quiet! You don't want

_____ to hear
            NAME OF PERSON YOU KNOW

us, do you?" I shook my head and made a muffled

_____ noise. He moved faster and faster until I
        SOUND

felt like a(n)_____, burning with desire. But just as
                SOMETHING HOT

I felt on the verge of _____, the door opened, and
                            VERB ENDING IN -ING

_____ walked into the closet. "Can I join
        WOMAN'S NAME

you?" she asked, slipping out of her _____.
                                            ARTICLE OF CLOTHING

"I heard you moaning '_____'
                            SOMETHING YOU WOULD SAY IN BED

from the hallway, and I had to see you in action." He nodded, and

I was too _____ to respond. I felt her hands
                EMOTION (ADJECTIVE)

slip up my _____ as she reached around his back.
                BODY PART

"Everything is better with three," she said.

CELEBRITY ENCOUNTER
Fill in the Spank:

Restaurant: _____

Male Actor: _____

Movie Featuring That Actor: _____

Sexual Activity (past tense): _____

Adjective: _____

Type of Residence: _____

Song Title: _____

Sexual Activity (verb): _____

Fictional Character: _____

Catchphrase of Fictional Character: _____

Verb Ending in -ING: _____

Something You Would Say to Seduce a Lover: _____

I was in my favorite restaurant, _____,
                                              RESTAURANT

when I saw him. I couldn't believe it—it was

_____! I'd had very dirty dreams
              MALE ACTOR

about his character in _____, so dirty
                              MOVIE FEATURING THAT ACTOR

that I had _____ on multiple occasions with
           SEXUAL ACTIVITY (PAST TENSE)

him in mind. Against all odds, he talked to me, and apparently

he found my _____ conversation thrilling, because
                ADJECTIVE

he invited me to his _____. There, he stripped off
                      TYPE OF RESIDENCE

his clothes in a sexy striptease set to _____.
                                              SONG TITLE

It was a fantasy come to life, and all I wanted to do was

_____, but he stopped me.
      SEXUAL ACTIVITY (VERB)

"You be _____," he prompted.
              FICTIONAL CHARACTER

"_____," I whispered,
      CATCHPHRASE OF FICTIONAL CHARACTER

and he moaned in my ear. "I didn't know you were into that,"

I said, taken aback by his response. "Oh yes," he said, "that

and _____." I pushed him onto the bed.
           VERB ENDING IN -ING

"_____"
      SOMETHING YOU WOULD SAY TO SEDUCE A LOVER

I growled.

SPANK BANK
Fill in the Spank:

Number: _____

Fabric/Material: _____

Body Part (plural): _____

Noise: _____

Body Part: _____

Exclamation: _____

Adjective: _____

Emotion (adjective): _____

Noise: _____

Noise: _____

Color: _____

Noun: _____

She hadn't expected her lover to have so many different floggers

and whips. "Why do you have _____ type(s) of whips in
                              NUMBER

here?" The room was cold against her bare skin. She saw a pair

of _____ cuffs hanging from the
       FABRIC/MATERIAL

ceiling. Her _____ perked up just
                  BODY PART (PLURAL)

seeing them. Her lover took a flogger down from the wall,

and then attached the cuffs to her. "Stand still," her lover said.

The flogger made a(n) _____ as it sailed
                              NOISE

through the air. It hit her exposed _____.
                                          BODY PART

"_____!" she screamed in surprise.
          EXCLAMATION

But the flogger also felt _____. She hadn't expected
                              ADJECTIVE

herself to get wet and _____ at the
                              EMOTION (ADJECTIVE)

very first swat. "Turn around," said her lover. The flogger sailed

through the air again. _____! _____!
                              NOISE   NOISE

Her skin started to turn _____ where the flogger fell.
                              COLOR

"Does it hurt?" asked her lover. "It feels like getting hit with a(n)

_____!" she cried. Her lover swung again. "Good."
      NOUN

BREAK-UP SEX
Fill in the Spank:

Number: _____

Insult: _____

Noun: _____

Something You Would Yell When Angry: _____

Number: _____

Adjective: _____

Something You Would Moan: _____

Piece of Furniture: _____

Object: _____

Adjective: _____

Insult: _____

Insult: _____

Body Part: _____

Sexy Verb Ending in -ING: _____

We were about _____ hour(s) into an argument, and it was
NUMBER

clear by this point that we were breaking up. His face was red

as he yelled, "_____!" I was so angry, I picked up
INSULT

his _____ and threw it against the wall.
NOUN

"_____!" I screamed. He marched
SOMETHING YOU WOULD YELL WHEN ANGRY

up to me until his face was only _____ centimeter(s) from
NUMBER

mine. "We're finished," he said. I nodded, my heart pounding.

"Good," he said, and without another word, he kissed me. His

hands were _____, all over my body. "One last time?"
ADJECTIVE

he asked. "Yes," I said, "_____." He
SOMETHING YOU WOULD MOAN

picked me up and we fell onto the _____,
PIECE OF FURNITURE

sending my _____ flying. He was rough, but
OBJECT

also _____ as he ripped at my clothes.
ADJECTIVE

"_____," he said. "_____!"
INSULT   INSULT

I yelled back. Then I thrust my _____ in his mouth
BODY PART

so he couldn't talk anymore. Break-up sex doesn't require talking

—it just requires _____.
SEXY VERB ENDING IN -ING

– 81 –

A ROYAL BEDDING
Fill in the Spank:

Adjective: _____

Animal: _____

Something You Would Say to a Queen: _____

Adjective: _____

Adjective: _____

Sexy Verb: _____

Something You Would Wear: _____

Noun: _____

Body Part: _____

Weapon: _____

Noise: _____

The Queen was in no mood to meet a suitor, but her advisor

had insisted. The suitor waltzed into her throne room, cocky

and _____. His attitude reminded her of a(n)
       ADJECTIVE

_____. He bowed deeply and said, "My
       ANIMAL

Queen. _____." She had no
         SOMETHING YOU WOULD SAY TO A QUEEN

use for marriage, but she did like the look of him, with

his _____ posture and his _____ eyes.
        ADJECTIVE   ADJECTIVE

The Queen opened her knees slightly, inviting him forward. "How

would you pay homage to your Queen?" she asked. "I would

_____," he said. He rushed to kneel at her feet. She stood
   SEXY VERB

up, her _____ shining in the sun. "Bend over
          SOMETHING YOU WOULD WEAR

my throne," she demanded, and he did it with the enthusiasm of

a(n) _____. When his body was prone and his
          NOUN

_____ was in the air, the Queen took a large
   BODY PART

_____ off the wall. She turned it so she could use the
   WEAPON

flat side, and then swung it with all her might. There was a

resounding _____ as it landed on his backside.
                 NOISE

"All hail the Queen!" he wailed.

BLIND DATE
Fill in the Spank:

Type of Residence: _____

Number: _____

Person's Name: _____

Man's Name: _____

Body Part (plural): _____

Type of Contraception: _____

Sexy Verb: _____

Body Part: _____

Body Part You Can Open: _____

Something You Would Moan: _____

Person's Name: _____

Person's Name: _____

Adjective: _____

Sexy Verb: _____

Verb Ending in -ING: _____

He was nothing to her but one more date in a long string of dates,

but she invited him back to her _____ anyway.
TYPE OF RESIDENCE

They were _____ minute(s) into making out when
NUMBER

she threw her head back and said, "Give it to me,

_____!" "Uh," he said, "it's actually
PERSON'S NAME

_____." "Right," she said, "sorry!" She used
MAN'S NAME

her _____ to draw him closer, fumbling
BODY PART (PLURAL)

with the _____ in her hurry
TYPE OF CONTRACEPTION

to _____. He quickly pushed his
SEXY VERB

_____ into her _____.
BODY PART   BODY PART YOU CAN OPEN

" _____!" she moaned. "Don't stop,
SOMETHING YOU WOULD MOAN

_____!" He quirked an eyebrow. "That's
PERSON'S NAME

not my name," he said. "Whatever," she breathed. "Why

don't I call you _____ instead? That will be
PERSON'S NAME

_____." "Whatever you want," he said, as he
ADJECTIVE

continued to _____. "As long as you don't stop
SEXY VERB

_____!"
VERB ENDING IN -ING

- 85 -

SUCK MY BLOOD
Fill in the Spank:

Man's Name: _____

Adjective: _____

Pickup Line: _____

Color: _____

Song Title: _____

Drink: _____

Adjective: _____

Noise: _____

Body Part: _____

Animal: _____

Sexual Activity (verb): _____

Something Dry: _____

I never understood why people thought vampires were so

sexy. At least, I never did until I met _____. He was

everything a vampire should be: dark, brooding, _____,

and European. The night we met, he saw me at the bar and said,

"_____." He might as well

have stripped off my _____ panties. After dancing to

_____ and drinking shots of

_____, I allowed him to take me out to the alley

to "taste" me. His breath was hot and _____ as

his lips traveled up and down my neck. "Bite me," I said. I heard

him breathe in sharply, his fangs ejecting with a _____.

He kissed the skin around my collarbone and opened his mouth

wide. "No, not there," I breathed. "Bite my _____." In

his hungry state, he could only grunt like a(n) _____. As

his teeth penetrated my skin, and I felt the first suck of his mouth,

I finally realized why everyone wanted to _____ with

vampires. Their hunger was pure. And his hunger was going to

drain me as dry as a(n) _____.

HOWLING AT THE MOON
Fill in the Spank:

Body Part: _____

Body Part: _____

Animal: _____

Something You Would Say in Bed: _____

Adjective: _____

Something You Would Say When Upset: _____

Noise: _____

Adjective: _____

Animal: _____

Animal Sound: _____

Part of Your House: _____

Adjective: _____

He was lying next to me in bed, kissing my _____ with a
                                           BODY PART

fierce longing. I felt his tongue lapping at my _____ and
                                                 BODY PART

I let out a sound like a(n) _____. His back was
                             ANIMAL

arched, and as he kissed down my body, I heard him mutter,

"_____." The moon came out from behind
  SOMETHING YOU WOULD SAY IN BED

a cloud, illuminating us both with _____ moonlight.
                                    ADJECTIVE

He sat up, his face wild. "Is tonight the full moon?" he asked.

He jumped out of bed. "_____!"
                        SOMETHING YOU WOULD SAY WHEN UPSET

I saw his shoulders arch and heard him cry "_____!"
                                             NOISE

His body began to transform right in front of me, from a(n)

_____ man into a wild _____. I
    ADJECTIVE   ANIMAL

cried out in shock. The beast, breathing heavily, made a(n)

_____ noise and then crashed
          ANIMAL   SOUND

through my _____, looking
            PART OF YOUR HOUSE

for _____ meat, but leaving me unharmed.
        ADJECTIVE

KISS AND A HAIRCUT
Fill in the Spank:

Woman's Name: _____

Something Soft: _____

Type of Toiletry: _____

Body Part: _____

Physical Description (adjective): _____

Color: _____

Noun: _____

Pickup Line: _____

Body Part: _____

Noun: _____

Type of Spa Service: _____

Clara's new hairdresser certainly had a gentle hand.

_____ ran her hands through Clara's
hair with such delicacy, it felt like being touched by

a(n) _____. Clara couldn't help but moan as
her hairdresser massaged _____ into her long
locks. Her hairdresser must have felt the electricity between them,

too, because she began to run her hands down Clara's neck and

shoulders, and finally across her _____. Clara shuddered
and turned the swiveling chair around. The woman was tall

and _____, with short _____ hair
and a tattoo of a _____ on her arm. The hairdresser
propped her hands on the chair and leaned in for a kiss.

"_____," Clara said, and the hairdresser
smiled. She ran her comb over Clara's _____, and Clara
got goose bumps all over. Then the hairdresser took some oils and

rubbed them into her palms, spreading _____-scented
oil over Clara's forearms. "Never mind the haircut," Clara said.

"How about a _____?"

DOWNWARD DOG
Fill in the Spank:

Number: _____

Body Part: _____

Type of Business: _____

Animal: _____

Type of Plant: _____

Sexy Verb: _____

Emotion (adjective): _____

Animal: _____

Body Part: _____

Article of Clothing: _____

Body Part: _____

Something You Would Say in Yoga: _____

"Breathe in," said my yoga instructor. "Now hold it for

_____ second(s)." I held my breath, and felt his hands on
NUMBER

my back, drawing up toward my _____. I couldn't
                                        BODY PART

help but exhale. It was a private lesson in a yoga studio above

a _____. "Now move into downward
        TYPE OF BUSINESS

_____," he said, and I lifted my tail toward
        ANIMAL

the sky. "Now crouch down into _____ pose," he
                                        TYPE OF PLANT

said, which put me on my back on the mat. He hovered over me.

"Now I'll show you _____pose," he said. I smiled,
                            SEXY VERB

feeling _____ as he lowered his body onto mine,
            EMOTION (ADJECTIVE)

grunting like a(n) _____. When he was hovering just
                        ANIMAL

inches from me, he licked my _____. "You've got
                                    BODY PART

sweat all over your _____," he said.
                            ARTICLE OF CLOTHING

"Let me show you a new position." He tilted my pelvis

until my feet were above my _____.
                                    BODY PART

"_____," he said. I took
    SOMETHING YOU WOULD SAY IN YOGA

another deep breath and let him move my body around

into every position he liked.

– 93 –

SELF-LOVE
Fill in the Spank:

Liquid: _____

Sex Toy: _____

Person's Name: _____

Piece of Furniture: _____

Song Title: _____

Something You Would Watch on TV: _____

Body Part: _____

Noun (plural): _____

Noun (plural): _____

Verb Ending in -ING: _____

Adjective: _____

Period of Time: _____

Emotion (adjective): _____

It was just me tonight—just me and my bottle of

_____. And we had a date with a(n)

_____ and with _____,

which is what I call my right hand. I lay back on the

_____, the lights dimmed, the stereo playing

_____. I turned on the TV so I

could watch _____,

which always put me in the mood. Slowly I reached down

and began to touch my _____. I moved

faster and faster, imagining _____ and

_____   _____.

As the heat began to build, I started to feel all _____.

This   wasn't   going   to   take   long.   It   had   been

_____ since I'd had the night to myself,

and I felt _____.

GOING UNDER COVER
Fill in the Spank:

Location: _____

Location: _____

Flavor: _____

Last Name: _____

Color: _____

Body Part: _____

Profession: _____

Man's Full Name: _____

Type of Drink: _____

Body Part: _____

Something Sweet: _____

Body Part: _____

Small Object: _____

Body Part: _____

My last few missions had taken me to Belfast, Argentina,

_____, and _____. But this was sure to be my
　　　LOCATION　　　　　　　LOCATION

hardest mission yet. I met him at his villa, under the pseudonym

_____ _____. I wore a
　　　　　FLAVOR　　　　　　　　　　LAST NAME

_____ wig, fake lashes, and a dress plunging so low, you
　　　COLOR

could see my_____. I was here to seduce
　　　　　　　　　　BODY PART

the rich _____,
　　　　　　　　　　　　　PROFESSION

_____. "Signora," he said, pouring
　　　MAN'S FULL NAME

me a glass of _____. I took a sip and
　　　　　　　　　　　TYPE OF DRINK

let my dress strap fall off my shoulder. He ran his hand over my

_____ lightly, transfixed by the softness of my skin.
　　BODY PART

I reached up to kiss him, and he tasted like _____.
　　　　　　　　　　　　　　　　　　　　　SOMETHING SWEET

I put one hand on his _____ while the other reached
　　　　　　　　　　　　BODY PART

around behind him, slipping into his pocket. There it was!

The flash drive, and also a _____. I kissed him
　　　　　　　　　　　　　SMALL OBJECT

harder as I picked his pockets, and he never noticed a thing.

Langley would be pleased. As he dropped his hands to my

_____, I realized I would be pleased too.
　　BODY PART

DARE TO DREAM
Fill in the Spank:

Attractive Celebrity: _____

Person You Have a Crush on: _____

Location: _____

Verb Ending in -ING: _____

Food: _____

Body Part (plural): _____

Sexy Verb Ending in -ING: _____

Famous Person: _____

Relative: _____

Object (plural): _____

Location: _____

Noun: _____

Adjective: _____

Animal: _____

Costume: _____

Something You Would Say in a Threesome: _____

Last night I had the most amazing dream. I was with

_____ and _____, and we
    ATTRACTIVE CELEBRITY   PERSON YOU HAVE A CRUSH ON

were in _____. We were _____,
           LOCATION   VERB ENDING IN -ING

when they turned to me at the same time and said, "Have you ever

tried being a human _____?" They wrapped me up between
                    FOOD

them, so I couldn't tell whose lips were on whose _____.
                                        BODY PART (PLURAL)

We started _____, but then _____ and
        SEXY VERB ENDING IN -ING   FAMOUS PERSON

_____ barged in and started throwing
        RELATIVE

_____ at us to get us to stop. I ran to
        OBJECT (PLURAL)

the _____, where I saw a(n) _____.
        LOCATION   NOUN

Strangely, I was so turned on by the sight of it, I felt my underwear

getting _____. Then a(n) _____ chased
        ADJECTIVE   ANIMAL

me back to the hotel, where I found my friends waiting to finish

our threesome. I took off my _____ outfit and started
                            COSTUME

stroking my new friends. "_____,"
                            SOMETHING YOU WOULD SAY IN A THREESOME

I said.

CLIMAX AND RESOLUTION
Fill in the Spank:

Body Part: _____

Body Part That Opens: _____

Number: _____

Number: _____

Something You Would Yell: _____

Song Title: _____

Body Part: _____

Body Part: _____

Something You Would Say to a Masseuse: _____

Insult: _____

Something You Would Scream: _____

I'd been thrusting my _____ into her
BODY PART

_____ for nearly _____ minute(s), but she
BODY PART THAT OPENS   NUMBER

was no closer to finishing. I couldn't seem to find her hot

spots. I had finished almost _____minute(s) ago, yelling
NUMBER

"_____!" as I climaxed. But I heard her
SOMETHING YOU WOULD YELL

humming _____, and I knew she
SONG TITLE

wasn't into it. Finally, my _____ brushed against her
BODY PART

_____, and her eyes lit up. "There!" she cried. "There?
BODY PART

Really?" I said. But I kept moving, and she started to moan.

"_____," she whispered. And
SOMETHING YOU WOULD SAY TO A MASSEUSE

then, "_____!" I wasn't sure where that came from, but I
INSULT

just kept moving. Finally, she exploded, trembling and screaming,

"_____!" I lay back, satisfied that
SOMETHING YOU WOULD SCREAM

I'd finally taken her all the way to the end. As her breath slowed

down, she looked over at me and smiled. "I hope we can do this

again sometime."